Thank you, Dearest Paul

Regii

STILL HERE

AUSTIN MACAULEY PUBLISHERS™

LONDON • CAMBRIDGE • NEW YORK • SHARJAH

ISBN 9789948794905 – (Paperback)
ISBN 9789948794912 – (E-Book)

Application Number: MC-10-01-1515337
Age Classification: 17+

First Published 2023
AUSTIN MACAULEY PUBLISHERS FZE
Sharjah Publishing City
P.O Box [519201]
Sharjah, UAE
www.austinmacauley.ae
+971 655 95 202

She wanted to be free in her soul, not caught up, not tied to her past life.

She was always caught up in tangles, up in knots.

She kept to herself, for the same reasons.

She spoke to herself a lot, dreamed of freedom and how wonderful it would be on her own.

She made plans, although she knew it would never exist, she made them, of when she grew up.

A quiet human sat in the corner, she read a lot for herself, to herself.

It was an escape from the harshness around her.

She felt everything, she adjusted, she existed, she gave in.

Only because she was made to feel lucky, at least she didn't die.

In the end, it's all we want and happiness.

When you lay your head weightlessly on your pillow at night.

No guilts, no fears, no wants so desperate that keeps us up all night.

That's all we want.

Right?

Fighting your own battles and overcoming obstacles.

Not others but your own.

Why take the key of others' houses and roam around?

When you still have roof to build over your own.

She sat on her desk, smiling within herself, the sun shone bright and it made her happy.

She thought of the vast fields, the green pastures, the dandelions all swaying choreographed by the breeze.
The birds in the air chirping so melodiously, like a sonnet, a choir.
The butterflies fluttering with their shades of beautiful, so quietly, yet their presence is known.
A honk of a passing car bought her back to reality, her tea sat cold in the cup, the sun still shone on her desk,
its warmth made her snuggle feeling inside.
She sat there, in the darkness of her room, drifting away to the chirping of the birds.

She waited on him at the dinner table, for the creak of the door as he opened,
he never came, just like other nights that turned into months and years.
How will we live? If I come home according to your convenience, he said every time.
But there are also others who earn for their family and yet make time to come home.
That's not like it, you have an answer for everything.
Step into my shoes, he always said, only then you will know the pressure of performing.
She stopped speaking, she stopped reacting.
Maybe he was right, she didn't know.

She had a hard exterior.
No one knew her so deeply.
She was known to be brash, so unbending.
Someone who takes her decisions like the coldest day you've
ever known.
So oblivious to feelings almost non-existent,
but she was not that, no she wasn't.
She was soft like the cotton in the fields, so flexible in her
approach, humility soared within her.
Always a help in hand, hurts when you hurt,
cries when you cry, feeds when you are hungry,
all that and more.
No one knew her enough that her hard exterior.

He told her to be ready at 8,
movie and dinner, it's a date.
Trying to make amends for his broken promises,
Still lasted in their second year of marriage.
She looked at the clock, 45 mins ago he was supposed to be
here.
But, again, no sign or message from him.
It became a norm, was she expecting the stars?
By now, even the empty night sky she came to love.

She was so used to unsteady,
vulnerable at every step,
hidden in layers of clothing yet her flesh was open for the
world to see.
Every story created on her by the world, who didn't even
know her as yet.
She was ripped apart every time she inhaled
and exhaled torment and berate
that both kept her alive,
the talk of the town, the city—she became.

She just kept covering up her body,
kept pulling the sleeves so her arms can't be seen.
Tugging her collar, pulling her scarf more tighter,
she was too embarrassed, from the marks that covered her.
Permanent scars were her permanent reminders.
Behind doors she saw them, she touched them,
they were beautiful, unique in their own designs.
Some on the surface, some deeper, like a pattern from a dress.
It was beautiful,
only wish someone could see it.

A little ray of hope she held, as the candle in her dark room
was snuffing away.
That she won't need to deal with demons every day, instead,
she can move ahead.
But they just sat by her, took every stride,
like a need, a necessity.
What would she be without all these thoughts?
Nothing, nothing at all… and that's what she was afraid of.

She was just 8, maybe, or still younger, when she was groped. She was kissed on her lips by another person.

A car stopped by her as she went to the shop, and a guy holding his penis outside, speaking in a language she didn't understand.

Thank God she got home safe. She told her mom, her mother made her go to the store again and told if he comes again, come and call her.

She agreed. She obeyed. Cause she was more scared of her mother than that person in the car.

But thankfully he never turned up.

So many occasions, different circumstances, men touched her, fondled her, and she got so scared.

But she had no family to speak to.

As she grew up, it never stopped. As she tried one day speaking to her family, she was blamed of lying and wrongfully standing to attract such people.

She got used to this even though it scared the life out of her inside.

It got norm, a way of life.

At such a young age, she lived so many lives, dodging death
or the wrath of death each day.

At such a young age, she used to think so terribly, something
she was not even supposed to be thinking.

She held conversations in her head and killed herself each day
and held mental funeral for herself each day,

just cause she wanted to be looked up with same kindness and
love as children of her age, not with disgust and a curse.

Inside, she was just a frightened soul, in a dark corner,
avoiding situations and circumstances that she was not even a
part of.

She was a fright, she was disgusted, it was sad she thought
this would be her future.

She longed each day for the night to come, so she could go to her bed, her place of comfort, especially when the lights went off.

She slept dearly.

Just being existent at her home was trouble enough for her.

Her mother couldn't stand the sight of her.

She was made to be disgusted and stank.

She never spoke and very seldom lay spoken to.

Even as she sat on the dining table to eat, she had to eat with her head down, and only with the given amount of food, if she took a little extra, her mother would stare wickedly on her.

She was made to feel that she 'owed' her mother, that she lived, and ate, and drank, and slept, and everything was to be paid back someday.

She would be glad that night came and she could go to her bed and just lay there.

And it came…

Her parents fought again that night, and between her siblings, she was always left alone and blamed for the fight.

Her mother and sister went off to the bedroom and slept.

And she and her dad and younger brother went to the other room.

Everyone had a bed, except her.

She slept in between two beds.

They started to fall asleep soon and she couldn't.

The room was cold and getting colder into the night.

A fragile body, was scared if she woke anyone up for a blanket to cover her body.

She fell asleep and woke up suddenly shaking, her body shaking uncontrollably.

She fell asleep again and woke up suddenly, her body shuddering.

She felt so sick, she waited for the morning this time.

So they would get up, and she would be warm again.

Her mind tried to keep awake, reading a book.

But her eyes slowly drooped,

escaping the reality of the world.

A rare instance, from the sleepless nights.

Today, her eyes gave in.

Did those tablets work?

I should take it every day, she thought to herself, at least sleep is something I can get, whether it's in peace or not, at least sleep is what I can get through those tablets.

It was 3:45 as she nodded off to a much-needed sleep.

She wished to talk to the stars, not just gaze at them in the night sky.

She wanted the moon, to secretly take her away.

To a land, that only existed for those who wanted to be there.

Away from longings, away from desires, away from greed, away from selfishness.

To the land of love, to the sky of pureness.

She was to pay back for been given birth, for the stitches her bearer had while she came into this world.

She was to pay back for all the pain her mother had to endure at the delivery table.

She was to pay back for all the work her mother did when she grew up.

She was to pay back for staying in her own house.

She was to back for the food she ate, even though it was monitored.

She was to pay back for being alive.

She was to pay back for surviving a trauma.

She did, and she still is…

She was a stranger in her own house.

No one spoke much to her, while she had so much to speak about.

Every message came to her in the form of passed on information, or just when the belt struck her for a mistake that was not hers.

She was spat at, looked down with disgust, cursed on her existence, and belted often.

She was woken up with shouting in her ears and swallowed her own vomit in fear.

She wanted to die each day, but she never did.

Or maybe, be handicapped, at least she would have got some love and attention.

But nothing happened.

She lived facing all of this alone, all alone.

As she cried herself to sleep.

It was another day, just like many others.

Her dark side began to surface,

the ugly feelings which she tried to hide.

The battles she started to fight mentally, and with herself, drowned her to the abyss.

She felt so sick from all of this.

The feelings that were never hers, but yet she felt it, so deep, that it struck as often as it could, and she would take it all, feel it all, battle it all, and then just lay exhausted near the drain. Tear stained and helpless, as if it were her battle to begin with.

She was wind, she was fire, she was a hurricane.

Like a typhoon she spun around, round and round,

damaging and destroying who came her way.

Plucking, and uprooting, and throwing away

all things, beautiful too, she thought she didn't deserve it, it

was not hers to keep.

Wrecking herself, till she was out of breath.

God! she knew she had to stop.

She couldn't.

She gave it all away.

She was instilled with so much hate, so much crime, so much

rage, and that's what made her so…

She sat on the kitchen floor catching her breath, panting so heavily from what happened a while ago.

The knife lay beside her feet.

She folded her knees close to her chest and hugged herself so tightly.

In pain from everywhere, only tears flowed freely without barriers.

Her mouth, her eyes, her cheeks burned from those tears, her head throbbed inside of her.

Her wrists were bleeding from the constant hitting of the knife earlier, she did not know the damage she had done.

She wished she could have done more, so she could see it and taste it, end it once and for all.

But she was still alive and experiencing more pain from the core of her body.

It was dark, as she slowly made her way to the bathroom and then to bed.

The last thing she did not do, as the new year began, was to write a resolution or even think about it.

It was not real just like Santa.

The yearly doldrums written down only to given an occasional peek when she cleaned her drawers.

She was much more than the piece of paper.

A mighty roar, a warrior in that battle, she completed the ticks every day, without writing any.

Milk and honey she longed, to pass through her lips.
The luxury sat in her kitchen cupboard, but she was denied it.
The taste of a sip of coffee she was accounted,
she had to sneak it in her room, but the aroma filled the house
and she got caught.
It was a crime if she ever let anything delicious pass through
her lips.
She was beaten blue, if she never asked anyone to have it
before her.
She longed, she desired.

She used to dream of the days she will be married, kids running around, dirtying the place, untidiness in her house, scattered toys, and boot marks on the floor.

Her man coming from work exhausted, but she would make it all okay for him, happy to be home.

Eating at the table with conversations that led nowhere, and the shouting, and bickering, and numerous *ssshhh's* that would follow.

She used to dream of going out with her family, laying on the beach while her kids played near.

Having thoughtful conversations with her man, lost into each other.

Opening up to homemade sandwiches, and crisps, and cold drinks from the soda machine, as they gather together from playing around.

The drive home, as kids would be asleep in the back seat, as she would slide her hands into his as he drove to the sun sinking on the horizon.

Tears flowed down her face, her skin felt hot and burning at the same time.

The mucus leaked out of her nose onto her lips, she didn't wipe it away.

She moaned with pain, nothing came out of her mouth, just moans of exhaustion, end of the rope, she didn't even wish for that knot to be there.

Please leave me—please let me die, she screamed inside of her.

She beat herself more and more mentally, emotionally, as she covered her ears harder to 'stop'.

It echoed loud, as she took a deep breath and she moaned louder.

It was like a competition, one of it to win, but both pushed its way with force.

And then slowly she began to calm down just like that, as she always did.

"Come," he told her, let's walk this together, you and me.

NO! I cannot, I don't think I can hold for long.

But why? he asked again.

Cause every time I stood up to walk, with every step I took, they cut pieces of me, peeled me, tore me, scraped me, I became non-existent.

They mocked me cause I kept falling, cause my mouth wouldn't open, my eyes were covered, they hung me on a stick and made me walk on glass.

I have nothing, I am nothing.

He looked at her.

"Come," he said again, stretching out his hand this time.

Let me carry you on this journey together.

We are all broken.
Some in pieces,
some in fragments.
We stand out because out hurt has shaped us,
into something,
into someone.
We wish for different.
Not realizing, this is different.
We can't even recognize ourselves in the mirror anymore.
To someone who we once were.
We look the same.
But we are so different.
Our brokenness.

www.ingramcontent.com/pod-product-compliance
Lightning Source LLC
Chambersburg PA
CBHW061328140726
47998CB00007B/2599